f

s

In the 13th century, Saint Louis decided to establish a port on the Mediterranean with the aim of reconquering the Holy Land. Consequently, the city of Aigues-Mortes was constructed *ex nihilo* on the swampy reaches of the Camargue. It was from this city that the king embarked on the Seventh Crusade.

** The terms followed by an asterisk are explained in the glossary at the end of the book.*

The keep*, called the Tour de Constance, along with the 1,634 meters of ramparts, flanked by twenty towers, were completed in less than fifty years. The homogeneous fortifications, built along the regular lines of bastides*, still surround the city.

Overleaf: aerial view of the city of Aigues-Mortes, from the north looking south.

Aigues-Mortes only experienced a brief period of prosperity. The city's decline began as early as the 14th century in the face of the silting up of the canals and the port and the competition from the port city of Marseille.

After the Repeal of the Edict of Nantes in 1685 and throughout the course of the *Ancien Régime,* the Tour de Constance was the largest Protestant prison in the kingdom.

Today, the city of Aigues-Mortes remains one of the finest and most well-preserved examples of medieval military architecture.

The rooftops of the town, the Porte des Remblais and the Tour de Constance as seen from the southwest front.

HISTORY

The French Royal Family and the Languedoc Seacoast

Philip Augustus, King of France from 1180 to 1223, sought the restoration of monarchical authority in his kingdom. This political agenda of reconquest was pursued in the French Midi from 1209 to 1271 — the foundation of Aigues-Mortes in 1240 was the most visible manifestation of this policy. To this day, the city monuments stand as a testament to royal sovereignty.

The King and the Count of Toulouse

Placed between an English Aquitaine and a Provence under the authority of the Holy Roman Emperor, a large part of the Languedoc was under the sway of Raymond VII, Count of Toulouse, whose family's power extended into Palestine through the Count of Tripoli. Such a powerful family would naturally vie with the French monarchy and even seek to free itself of its distant authority.

Using religion as a pretext, the Kings of France ordered the Crusade against the Albigensians from 1209 to 1229 as a way of making inroads into the eastern confines of the Count's domains. There they established the senechalsy of Beaucaire, then that of Carcassonne at the head of which were placed royal administrators from Paris, loyal to the King instead of to local feudal lords. Naturally the Count and his supporters felt threatened by this new balance of power, which indicated the establishment of the basis for a centralized royal authority and a diminution of their ancestral rights. On several occasions, notably in 1240 and in 1242, they revolted.

The upheavals calmed down after the death of Raymond VII in 1249, when the county passed into the hands of Alphonse of Poitiers, the brother of Louis IX, then King of France. The region was finally annexed by the Crown in 1271.

Statue of Saint Louis, or King Louis IX, dating back to the 19th century. Notre-Dame-des-Sablons, Aigues-Mortes.

The King Thwarts Aragonese Expansion

At the beginning of the 13th century, King James I of Aragon, Count of Barcelona and Roussillon, established a foothold upon the Languedoc coastline when he assumed the title of Seigneur of Montpellier. His presence complicated the established feudal system, since it constrained a king to render homage to another king — as in the case of Aquitaine — thus exacerbating political tensions. This led James I to forge a series of political and personal alliances that enabled him to lay a claim to Carcassonne; he also attempted to have the county of Provence pass into his family.

After 1240, Louis IX fortified the city of Carcassonne to confront this expansionist policy. In 1245, he also countered the matrimonial projects of James I of Aragon by according the hand of the heiress of the county of Provence to his brother, Charles of Anjou. In 1248, the Treaty of Corbeil resolved the issues between France and Aragon concerning the western part of Languedoc.

Thereafter, James' ambitions were confined to the islands in the Mediterranean. Louis IX reasserted his rights in the seigniory of Montpellier: in 1255, he managed to gain the allegiance of the bishop of Maguelone, thus disregarding certain prerogatives of the Holy See. He then compelled the King of Aragon to render homage to this prelate, who, from that time on, remained loyal to Louis.

A Foothold on the Mediterranean

Louis IX was the first King of France to dispose of a means of access onto the Mediterranean. At the time of the decline of Muslim power, an increasing number of Christian vessels navigated between Barcelona, Genoa and Venice and the coast of North Africa and the Levant. Any great power required a presence on those shores as the major Western powers attempted to control its maritime traffic.

But it was not merely base commerce that necessitated access: an accomplished ruler must also serve the Christian faith, notably in its struggle for the liberation of Jerusalem and the Holy Sepulchre. Louis IX, who embodied the virtues of the good Christian prince, took the cross twice. His successors attempted to follow in his footsteps until the middle of the 14th century.

The Crusades of Saint Louis

In December 1244, Louis IX took the cross. He embarked from Aigues-Mortes on 25 August, 1248 for Cyprus, then Egypt. Soon after his arrival, he took Damietta but his army was defeated at Mansourah, in April of 1250 and he was taken prisoner. Once liberated, he remained in Palestine until 1254 where he supervised the construction of Frankish strongholds. The King departed from Aigues-Mortes once again, on July 1, 1270, and headed for the Tunisian coast. He died at Carthage soon afterwards (on August 25th), after falling victim to the plague.

Cover of a schoolboy's exercise book, around 1900 (private collection).

Saint Louis sets off on crusade on the 25th of August, 1248. Miniature, 1330-1340 (Paris, Bibliothèque Nationale de France).

The City of Saint Louis

Around 1240, Louis IX undertook the construction of a city at the furthest limits of his kingdom — an arm of the Rhone, which flows into the Mediterranean near the town of Le

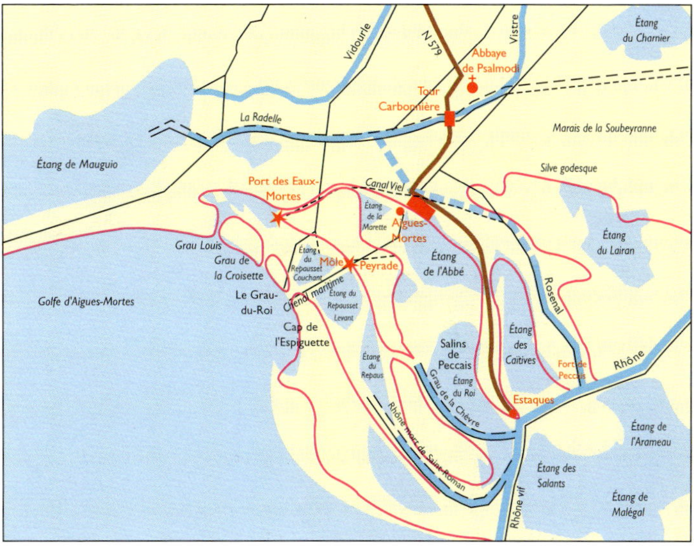

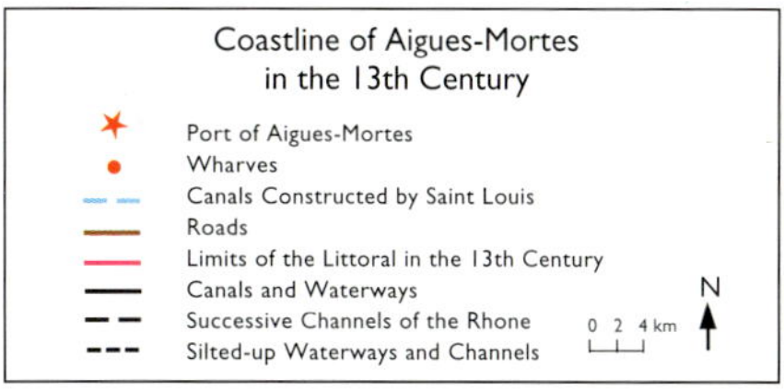

Grau-du-Roi, separated France from the Provençal lands owing allegiance to the Holy Roman Empire. The contours of the coastline at that period were similar to those which exist today: sand banks, which were gradually silting up, enclosed a lagoon open to the sea which gave off onto another series of lagoons. Most of this region was held by the Benedictine Abbey of Psalmodi, founded in the 8th century upon an island in the middle of the wetlands. In 1226, there was mention made of a Port des Eaux-Mortes, located at the point where one lagoon opened onto another (the Etang de l'Abbé, or "Abbot's Lagoon"), used by merchants from Montpellier and Marseille. It was on the edge of this lagoon, on a sandy wasteland between the port and the abbey, that Saint Louis decided to found his city.

The Founding of a City

On the King's orders, construction began with the erection of the *Grosse tour du Roi,* later named the Tour de Constance. Completed in 1248, its purpose was symbolic as well as functional: its beacon served as a guide for sailors and its imposing mass asserted the sovereign authority of the King. At the foot of this tower, a castle, long since disappeared, was constructed; a palisade surrounded the whole.

At the time of the castle's construction, the King entered into extensive negotiations with the Abbot of Psalmodi in order to obtain the cession of lands which he wished to confer upon his city. A formal agreement was established in 1248.

Under the protection of the rapidly established fortress, the King set out the foundations for his model city. As early as 1246, he endowed the still meagre population with an extremely advantageous charter. No city in the region enjoyed such extensive liberties. It served both a means of attracting settlers as well as an ultimate demonstration of royal munificence.

At the centre of the city is the parish church of Notre-Dame-des-Sablons, completed before 1260. It gives off directly onto the main square, which forms its parvis. Directly opposite was the magistrate's house, where the town hall is now located. We know very little about the privately-owned buildings since many of them were built with perishable materials due to the dearth of quarries in the area. For a long time, the population was concentrated in the western part of the city. Its grid plan, typical of bastides, with streets leading to the central square, is unique in eastern Languedoc. In the eastern part of the city there stretched a more open space, occupied only by a Franciscan convent and the town cemetery, to which a hospital was added in 1346.

The Church of Notre-Dame-des-Sablons as seen from the Place Saint-Louis.

Links with the Interior

The fortification of the city was an integral part of the King's plans but other projects took precedence, namely the immediate necessity of linking the city with its inland neighbours and the major centres of commerce. Before the end of Louis IX's reign in 1270, Aigues-Mortes was linked by waterway with Arles and Montpellier by means of two canals, or *roubines*, along the Rhone and the Etang de Mauguio. They also served to convey the bulk of the stone needed to construct the walls of the city. Additionally, the road leading from the abbey of Psalmodi to Nimes was extended to Aigues-Mortes, with the addition of the Pont de la Carbonnière, bridging the Vistre, upon which a tower was constructed. This series of works revealed the objective of the King: to make his city an important link in the European commercial routes between Provence and Languedoc, the Rhone axis with the fairs of Champagne, and the Mediterranean.

A Well-Situated Outer Harbour

Although Louis IX ordered a vast amount of construction in the city of Aigues-Mortes, the

Chargement des navires ("The Loading of the Ships"). Miniature, 1352 (Paris, Bibliothèque Nationale de France).

port area was relatively neglected. Many of the ports in the middle of the 13th century owed their success to natural advantages rather than man-made ones. The lagoon upon which the original port of Eaux-Mortes was situated was still largely open to the sea and offered seagoing vessels a deep moorage, sheltered from winds and currents. From this anchorage, merchandise was conveyed inland by flat-bottomed boats called *caupols*.

It was at this spot that, in 1248 and 1270, the ships that were to transport Saint Louis and his crusaders assembled. Thus, the symbiotic relationship of city and outer port was established — a model also found in the maritime cities of Languedoc, Narbonne and Montpellier.

Thanks to Louis IX's generous patronage, as his reign drew to a close the town of Aigues-Mortes, nestled at the foot of a royal fortress, was already in possession of a municipal body, some territories, a port and routes for communication and commerce. Still, it remained an unfortified city with a sparse population.

A Crusader Port

Already in 1239, crusaders were taking ship from the port which had sprung up previously, in spite of the insalubrious climate of Eaux-Mortes.

Long before the departure of Louis IX in 1248, equipment and provisions were being stockpiled at Aigues-Mortes in anticipation of the eventual embarkation. But the France of the 13th century was by no means a naval power and, as early as 1246, Saint Louis had to apply to Marseille, Venice and Genoa for the rental or purchase of ships while the port cities were themselves chartering vessels. Finally, 1,800 vessels met at Cyprus in 1249, but only thirty-eight had left Aigues-Mortes with the King.

In 1270, the crusaders were all summoned to this port, where the facilities for receiving them were non-existent. Quarrels erupted and the King, who was spending his last days before departure at Saint-Gilles, was forced to come early to reestablish order. Additionally, the available places on board were limited. Some crusaders went as far as soliciting papal intervention, others, rejected on all sides, took to piracy.

The City after 1270

The successors of Saint Louis did not content themselves with merely pursuing the existing work in progress on the fortifications. They took on the additional task of establishing a port closer to the city precincts. In 1272, in order to further these two projects, Philip III engaged Guillaume Boccanegra. This former captain was well-known in the port, where he appeared as early as 1249 as a representative of the Genoese. In fact, many Italians came to do business and then stayed to take up residence and many of the first town magistrates were Lombards by birth.

The Ramparts

Construction of the city walls began in the north. However, at the time of the death of Boccanegra in 1274, the work had not progressed much. In 1286, the war between France and Aragon over the affair of the Sicilian Vespers erupted and Admiral Roger de Loria launched an offensive upon the still-unfortified city. With the aim of cutting off French supply lines, he commanded several raids upon the coast of Aigues-Mortes and made off with several ships anchored in the port. Perhaps such a disaster increased the urgency of the construction — at any rate the fortifications were completed by the end of the 13th century, including the Tour Carbonnière, which commands the northern approach to the city, the only one by land.

France's Mediterranean Port

In order to facilitate port access, the work was expedited. In 1278, the offshore bar situated to the south of Aigues-Mortes was pierced and a stone jetty, the Peyrade, was built. The main advantage of this new site was to move port activity closer to the city precincts. With the aid of the new channels, galleys and other flat-bottomed vessels could sail right up to the city. That same year, Philip III compelled the Italian merchants to transfer their residences from Montpellier to Nimes, which would depend upon Aigues-Mortes as its port.

Northeast front, city-side, as seen from the Tour de Constance; from left to right, the Porte de la Gardette, the Tour du Sel, the Porte Saint Antoine, the Tour de la Mèche and Tour de Villeneuve.

This move did not have the desired result but it did have one consequence, that of obliging seagoing traffic to pass through Aigues-Mortes when entering or departing the kingdom in the south, instead of going by way of the *graus*, or channels, which depended on Montpellier. This measure had both political and economic repercussions upon the port city's activity. Thereafter, the warehouses of Aigues-Mortes housed spices and other commodities from the East, as well as merchandise from the fairs of Champagne, and fine wool from England which passed through Aquitaine and Languedoc on their way to Italian markets.

Territorial Expansion

Finally, the successors of Saint Louis took it upon themselves to increase the resources of the inhabitants by increasing the territory of the city. The endowment of property made by Louis IX was of limited usefulness: the approximately 1,800 hectares of sandy terrain constituted a meagre agricultural domain. In 1269, the King induced the Templars to cede a forest west of Aigues-Mortes to him. Then the Hospitaller Order left a neighbouring forest to Philip III. Thus, in 1272, the city's territories stretched as far as the Etang de Mauguio. Finally, in 1290, in the process of a negotiation with the Seigneur d'Aimargues et d'Uzès, Philip the Fair acquired the salt

Southwest front, outer face; from right to left, the Tour de la Poudrière, Porte de l'Arsenal and Porte de la Marine.

marshes of Peccais for the city. From that time onwards, the city of Saint Louis, characterized by its distinctive ramparts and the port, was also irrevocably linked with salt-making. All in all, it took sixty years to endow Aigues-Mortes with formidable fortifications and adequate port facilities, and provide it with as a large a land base as possible, taking into account the age-old rights of the Abbey of Psalmodi to the marshland, a claim that the rulers of the 13th century were hesitant to question.

But already the principal obstacle to decisive expansion had reared its head: located too far inland from the edge of the pools and too close to the mouth of the Petit-Rhône where its silt is deposited, the port of Môle filled slowly but inexorably with sand, to the point of endangering access for ships requiring a deep draught. Extensive work on a permanent basis was deemed necessary in order to maintain the accessibility and activity of the port and in the end, the royal will yielded to the forces of nature.

Southeast front, outer face; from right to left, the Porte des Cordeliers and Porte de la Reine.

Decline of the Port, Prestige of a Royal City

The short-lived apex of Aigues-Mortes' glory occurred around the turn of the 13th and early 14th centuries. From 1320 onwards, complaints about the need to land at this sand-bound port increased.

Subsequent attempts to remedy the situation remained ineffectual and the bid by

Jacques Coeur to make Aigues-Mortes the base for his trade with the Levant in 1423 ended in failure. The *coup de grâce* occurred in 1481 when Marseille was acquired by France and finally, in 1484, the monopoly of Aigues-Mortes was rescinded, marking the end of overseas commerce; the port was then relegated to being a mere coastal navigation stopover.

Nevertheless, the loyal city remained the object of royal solicitude. The massacre of the Burgundians in 1421 testified to the loyalty of the city which held out and only fell into the hands of opponents of the Crown by ruse or treason. But all attempts at major expansion were inhibited by the epidemics of sickness endemic to marshlands, as well as the lack of agricultural resources on this narrow stretch of land exposed to the floods and caprices of the Rhone and the Vidourle rivers. In spite of this, the imposing royal fortress retained its prestige and it was there that, in July 1538,

The channel which runs from Aigues-Mortes to the sea, with, in the background, the northwest front of the ramparts.

Francis I and the Emperor Charles V met to resolve their differences amidst great pomp and splendour.

Aigues-Mortes and the Protestants

Calvinism took root in Aigues-Mortes in 1560 and the town became a coveted stronghold during the Wars of Religion. In 1575,

The Protestant Prisoners of the Tour de Constance

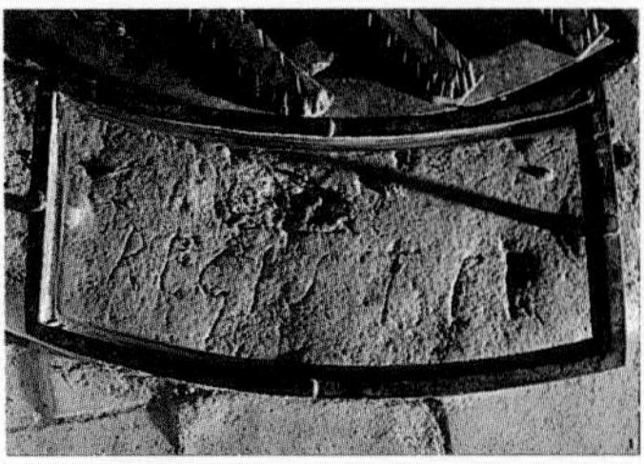

Register (resist), graffiti attributed to Marie Durand, carved into the sill of the roundel in the upper chamber of the Tour de Constance.

The Edict of Nantes, "perpetual and irrevocable", was indeed revoked in 1685. It was the beginning of a stringent repression of Protestantism, which met solid resistance in Languedoc and the Cévennes, resulting in the War of the Camisards at the beginning of the 18th century. From 1686 onwards, the Tour de Constance, in addition to the other towers of the fortress, were appropriated as a prison for Huguenots.

In 1705, the Camisard leader Abraham Mazel, along with sixteen of his companions, managed to escape from the tower by dislodging a stone from an arrow slit. After 1715, the tower was reserved for women — mostly poor natives of the Cévennes — who were imprisoned because of their Protestant beliefs or simply for having participated in a religious assembly. Their number varied but never exceeded thirty-eight. The conditions of their detention were difficult in the extreme: humidity, darkness and cold during the winter, with only rare outings on the terrace. Some died and some infants were born there. Several recanted and others were pardoned.

Marie Durand was a person of unshakable faith, convictions and energy. A native of Ardèche, she was arrested very young, with the aim of forcing her brother, a preacher, to turn himself in to the authorities. He was hanged in 1732, but she remained imprisoned for another thirty-six years, in 1768.

She is traditionally credited with the inscription of the word *Register* (Resist) upon the ledge of the roundel of the upper chamber. It later became a battle cry for the recognition of the freedom of conscience.

Tablet installed in the courtyard of the Governors's residence on 30 August, 1968, commemorating the bicentennial of the liberation of the Protestant prisoners. The bas-relief includes a galley, prison bars, a Huguenot cross and the words, *In memory of the Huguenot prisoners, and of all who "resisted" for their faith and for freedom of conscience.*

Huguenot troops took over the city, destroying the Convent of the Cordeliers and the Chapel of the Pénitents Gris.

After the peace of May 1576, Aigues-Mortes was declared one of eight secured towns and became a Protestant haven for forty-seven years. However, the city was delivered up to Louis XIII by its governor when the King laid siege to it, on the 22 August, 1622. The Counter-Reformation was in full force: the Capuchin order was established and the destroyed religious edifices restored; still, the two religious communities managed to coexist in relative peace. Upon the Revocation of the Edict of Nantes in 1685, the Tour de Constance was converted into a prison where Huguenots sentenced to death or the galleys were incarcerated. After the escape of the Camisard leader Abraham Mazel in 1705, only women were imprisoned there, notably Marie Durand, who survived there for thirty-eight years.

The Town's Revival

In the 18th century, definitive improvements were made. In 1725, a channel was dug between Aigues-Mortes and Le Grau-du-Roi. In 1747, the swamps were drained and, in 1772, construction began upon the canal of Beaucaire, which was completed in 1811. Then the Vidourle River was diverted towards the coast (1822-1847). But the city benefited above all from the phylloxera crisis that hit the French Midi around 1875 — a vineyard was created in the surrounding sands, which provided protection from the parasite, generating profit and growth for the city, which began to outgrow its fortifications. Beginning in the 1850s, the fashion of sea-bathing began to attract city-dwellers and created an additional source of profit for Aigues-Mortes, further facilitated by the railroad link established with Nimes in 1873.

In 1892, in an excess of nationalism, the Massacre of the Italians drew attention to the arduous labour of salt-making.

Its walls, rising up over the sandy terrain, have charmed many a visitor: Châteaubriand, Dumas, Mérimée, and Frédéric Bazille have all fallen under its spell.

Layout of Aigues-Mortes, taken from an atlas of fortified towns of Languedoc. Engraving, 18th century (Paris, Bibliothèque Nationale de France).

Chronology

1226 First reference to the Port des Eaux-Mortes.

1239 Crusaders set off from the Port des Eaux-Mortes.

Around 1240 The foundations of Aigues-Mortes are laid by the king.

Beginning of the construction of the Tour de Constance.

1246 Louis IX grants a charter of privileges to the inhabitants of Aigues-Mortes.

1248 The king negotiates with the Abbey of Psalmodi for the exchange of the territories of Aigues-Mortes with some land near Sommières. Aigues-Mortes is linked to the Rhone by the lengthening of an old arm of the river and to the lagoon, the Etang de Mauguio with the drilling of the Grande Roubine.

Louis IX sets off for the Seventh Crusade from Aigues-Mortes.

Before 1260 Construction of Notre-Dame-des-Sablons.

1269 Westward expansion of the territory of the city.

1270 Departure of Louis IX for the Eighth Crusade. He dies in Tunisia before Carthage.

1272 Philip III the Bold contracts with Guillaume Boccanegra for the construction of the ramparts and the conversion of the port. More expansion in the west.

1275 Creation of the port of Môle, of its levee (La Peyrade) and the canal that unites it with the city.

1286 The port is raided by Roger de Loria and the Aragonese.

1291 Philip IV exchanges various revenues with the Lord of Aimargues and Uzès for the salt marshes of Peccais to be ceded to Aigues-Mortes.

Towards 1300 Construction of the ramparts and of the Tour Carbonnière is completed.

1346 Foundation of a hospital.

1421 War between the Armagnacs and the Burgundians. Destruction of the castle and massacre of the Burgundians.

1423 Aigues-Mortes becomes the home port of Jacques Cœur's fleet.

1447 Following the silting up of the port, Jacques Cœur moves his fleet to Marseille.

1464 The king revokes the ruling that all merchants entering or leaving the kingdom pass through Aigues-Mortes.

1481 Marseille becomes French and Aigues-Mortes enters into a period of inexorable decline.

1538 Meeting between François I and Charles V, which seals the reconciliation of the two rulers.

1575-1576 The Wars of Religion. Aigues-Mortes becomes one of the eight southern Huguenot strongholds.

1622 The Protestant governor surrenders the city to Louis XIII.

1686 After the Revocation of the Edict of Nantes, Protestants are incarcerated in the Tour de Constance.

1705 The dramatic escape of Abraham Mazel.

1725 Extension of the canal of Aigues-Mortes to the sea and renovation of Le Grau-du-Roi.

1768 Liberation of the last Protestant women prisoners.

1772 Beginning of the work on the canal of Beaucaire.

1811 Dismantling of the fortress; the Governor's Residence is allocated for the Customs authorities.

1903 The fortifications and the Governor's Residence are classified as historical monuments.

1986 The Customs authorities relinquish the Governor's Residence. The National Register of Historical Monuments and Sites undertakes the restoration of the building. Installation of an elevator in the Tour de Constance.

Detail: *The South Face of the ramparts*, by Frédéric Bazille, oil on canvas, 1867 (Montpellier, musée Fabre).

TOUR OF THE CITY

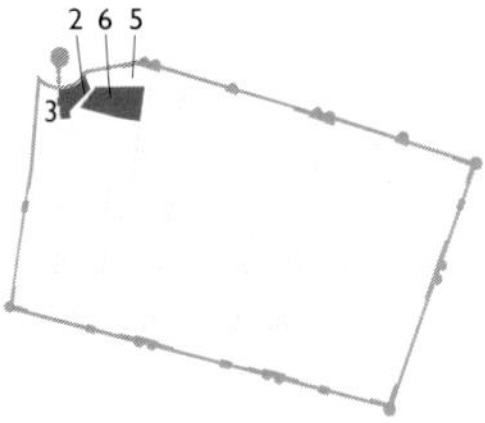

The military quarters of the fortress occupies the north-west corner of the city and comprises the Tour de Constance, the barracks, the Governor's Residence and the parade ground.

The parade ground[5] is a vast, roughly rectangular space of approximately 1,740 square meters bounded on the west by the circumvallation of the Governor's Residence and on the east by the Rue Jean-Jaurès.

The barracks[6] are located in the southwest corner of the parade ground. They were built between 1746 and 1750, on the site of the older ones. Until the 17th century, the town was responsible for the maintenance of the garrison; later on, the municipality was freed from that charge but was required in exchange to build the barracks. Its successive incarnations, notably as a police barracks, then as a hotel-restaurant, have left their traces upon the original structure.

The circumvallation[2], erected in 1624, originally encircled the Governor's Residence; today only two of the original three sides of the wall remain. The first includes a covered watchpath and a parapet* armed with loopholes* for shooting. The second, with a north-south orientation, provides access, via a large portal, to the Governor's residence. This wall does not possess a passage but it does have arrow slits at eye level. A round watchtower, or barbican* topped by a cupola presides over the angle where the two sections of wall join. The whole, covered with bossage*, seems to have been constructed with materials recovered from earlier medieval constructions, such as the barbican which once protected the Porte de la Gardette, or the La Peyrade jetty, a constituent element of the port.

The Governor's Residence

The Governor's Residence[3] is accessed by crossing the forecourt, circumscribed by the 17th-century circumvallation upon which a memorial inscription commemorates the struggle of the Protestants who were victims of past intolerance.

The barracks, Governor's Residence and the watchtower of the enclosing wall as seen from the Place d'Armes.

The construction of the building is hard to analyze as it is the product of numerous reworkings during the 16th and 17th centuries. It is a large, rectangular structure with four storeys — the second shorter than the others. The façades are classically decorated and the rear façade features an outwork containing a stairwell.

The bridge, the Governor's Residence, the *mur conque*, enclosing wall, and the barracks, as seen from the terrace of the Tour de Constance.

Until recently, this building was used by the Customs authorities. In 1986, restoration undertaken by the regional Association for the Conservation of Historical Monuments *(Conservation régionale des monuments historiques)* enabled the building to regain more of its original dimensions, as determined by 19th-century sources.

The history of this building is a complicated one. The residence was built on the site of the King's residence which had been destroyed by fire in 1421 and then rebuilt. A text dating back to 1542 situates the King's residence (or *Maison du Roi*) as "immediately adjoining the Tour de Constance". Documents from the end of the 17th century continue to mention the Maison du Roi — could it be the "old château" mentioned in a 1622 text?

Façade overlooking the front courtyard of the Governor's Residence, demarcated by the surrounding wall.

On the oldest maps of the period which mention Aigues-Mortes, one can make out a construction which the Tour de Constance gives on to, with a polygonal surrounding wall in three parts, fitted with two bartizans*. One remains, dating back to 1624, and it is known that the building was undergoing renovations in 1662.

The surrounding wall and its watchtower, topped by a cupola.

Unfortunately, there are no further sources which would make the succession of structures clear; the next sources are from the 18th century. The wall uniting the two parts of the medieval fortifications, behind the Tour de Constance, is referred to as the *mur conque*. This concave wall, along with the repair of the bridge of the Tour de Constance and some reworking of the tower parapets probably date back to the end of the 16th century.

Preceding pages: a view of the Governor's residence from the rear, including the interior courtyard and the 17th-century stairwell added onto the 16th-century façade.

The northern area of the fortress is the one which has undergone the most modifications in the modern era, to the point of being totally transformed; it was necessary to adapt it for more modern implements of war, notably cannon and rifles.

The entrance to the residence is made through an imposing central doorway, framed by Ionic pilasters*. Upon being admitted, one crosses two vaulted halls, the only remaining vestiges of the earlier lodgings, installed here by the administrators of the monument. The first, barrel-vaulted*, constitutes the principal means of access to the building. To the rear one can discern a rectangular stairwell with four newels, dated 1660-1670. The second chamber, with groin vaulting, gives off onto the interior courtyard of the residence. The stairway, the most splendid feature of the residence, leads up to three storeys of varying height which remain closed to the public for the moment. There is also a corkscrew staircase*, which has been added within a cylindrical turret on the northern face of the building, it currently leads to the covered watchpath.

Northeast view of the upper levels of the Tour de Constance.

When entering the interior courtyard, restored at the beginning of the 1980's, one can only partially perceive the aspect it presented in the 17th century. Then, it was further defined by an edifice of east-west orientation, and yet another was appended to the medieval walls. The disposition of this area in the 13th century is totally unknown today, since we are unaware of the means which linked this courtyard to the Tour de Constance. This space has been adapted for the presentation of special events in the summer months.

Rectangular stairwell, Governor's residence.

The Tour de Constance

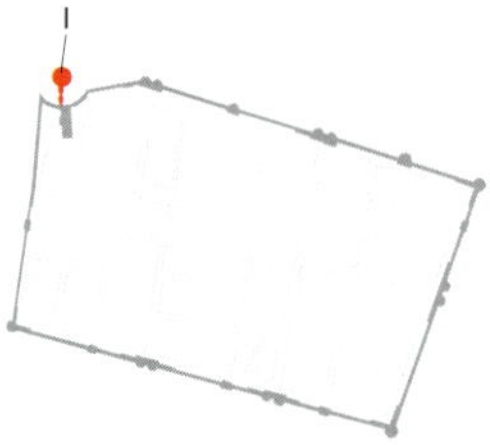

The Tour de Constance[1], completed in 1248, consists of an enormous cylinder with a sloped footing*. This work, done in a homogeneous and somewhat refined style, was executed in one fell swoop. The tower is thirty meters high, capped with a turret eleven meters tall and measures twenty-two meters in diameter. There are two entrances, one to the north, the other on the south side.

The foundations rest on deeply entrenched pilings to ensure stability on such swampy land. The construction is of filled bond*. The middle bond on the facings carries no bossage or mason's marks*, unlike the rest of the 13th-century constructions. The stone might have come from the quarries of Castillon-du-Gard, around twenty kilometers away, northwest of Beaucaire.

The layout of the entrance today is of recent origin. The bridge with three arches along which the visitor may roam is a modern conceit, as is the wall passage which traverses the *mur conque*. The parapet is two meters tall and is outfitted with loopholes* and rifle slits.

What was the original layout of this tower? The building was surrounded by a circular moat and an embankment. The moat was spanned with a wooden gangway, which could be taken up when the town was threatened.

This tower was certainly not isolated. In fact, it constituted the defensive structure for a larger dwelling, and secured the main access to that castle. Contrary to what has been asserted in the past, there is no evidence of it having been used as a habitation. For example, there are no latrines* on the first level, and the tradition of there being a "King's oratory" is quite probably apocryphal.

Little is known about the older castle. Sources attest to the presence of a castellan in 1249: Jean Porcheron is referred to as the "castellan of the Lord and King of France". Be that as it may, from the beginning of the 14th century until the French Revolution, the tower was used as a prison.

Vertical cross-section of the Tour de Constance, north-south orientation: bridge with three arches, dungeon, lower chamber, and terrace topped by a turret. Aquarelle by the architect Louzier, 1891 (Paris, Médiathèque du Patrimoine).

The name of the tower appears later and does not refer to a particular person, but rather to its architectural aspect. Previously called the "great tower" (or *grosse tour*), it comprises a dungeon, or oubliette*, a lower chamber, an upper chamber and a terrace dominated by a turret. The various levels are reached by a corkscrew* staircase constructed within a cylindrical stairwell affixed to the side of the structure, lit by three archers' loopholes*. A fourth opening provides light for the polygonal lantern, incomplete and since altered, which completes the whole.

The builders had planned to utilize the six-meter thick walls for the bulk of the passageways and basic facilities, leaving the interior spacious and unencumbered,

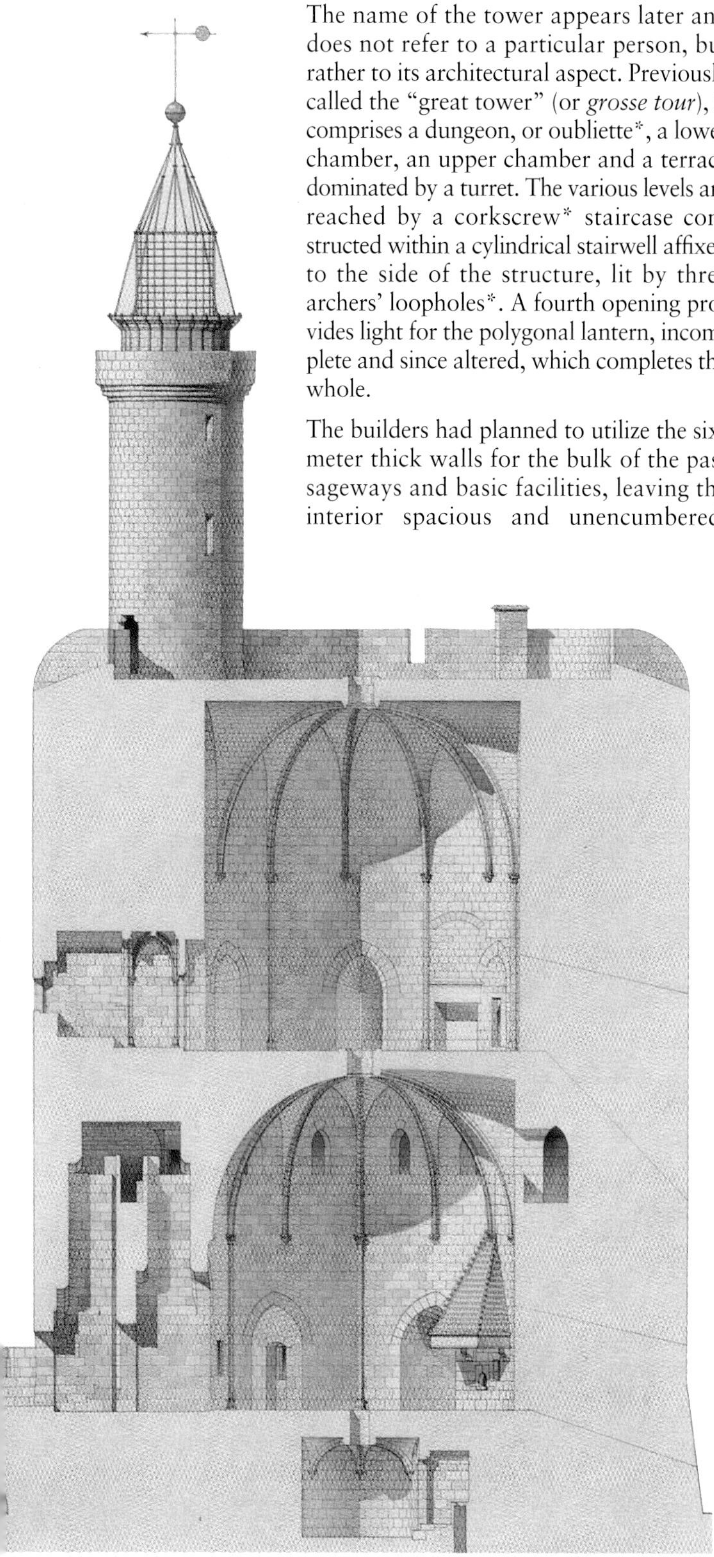

Lower chamber
of the Tour de Constance.

reserved for the chambers. Within them are ensconced the chimney flues, the well which gives onto the lower chamber, the watch-paths and passages and, off the upper chamber, a cistern which collected water from the terrace. Off the lower chamber are built-in closets and the entrance to the stairway. Also, an elevator, installed in 1986, now allows access from the lower chamber directly to the terrace.

The **dungeon** is not open to the public. Circular in shape, it has a ribbed vault with six spandrels with an open ring-shaped keystone which can be seen in the center of the lower chamber and constitutes the oubliette's sole access. The presence of latrines indicates that this place, normally reserved for supplies, once also served as a prison.

The **lower chamber,** with its circular layout, has a vault with twelve spandrels with ribs that end alternately in decorated sorbels* and polygonal colonnettes. As with the dungeon, the annular keystone links this room with the upper chamber. Four loopholes* open onto the exterior. Access is gained by a double door on the north side. A wooden portcullis* secured the interior door. The floor is made up of large paving stones.

In 1868, the construction of a chimney with an oven necessitated the destruction of one of the colonnettes. The design of the hood seems to have been adapted from an earlier chimney. There are also a few cupboards built into the wall.

The lower chamber is well-suited for defensive purposes as one can view it from a circular passageway with access from eleven arched doorways constructed within the mass of the wall in the higher part of the chamber. Thus, visitors passed through the northern entrance into the room where they were inspected and, if they proved to be hostile, they were repelled from the passageway overlooking it. Access to the castle was also possible from the south door that was also defensible from the covered watchpath above in case the other points of defense encountered this far did not hold out.

The watchpath commands the two entrances; it was from here that the operation of the portcullises and the murder-hole are controlled. A sole loophole* with a northern ori-

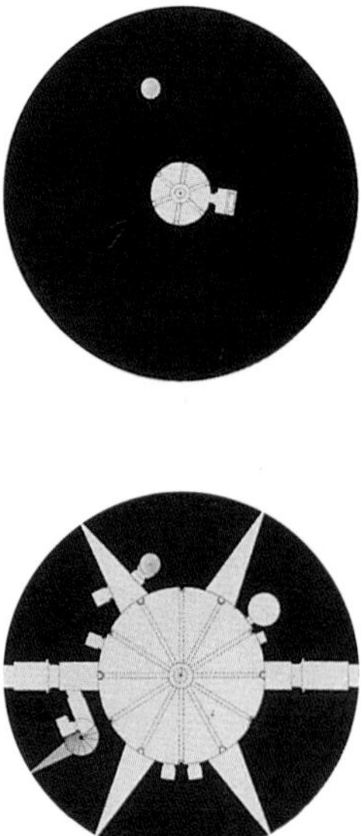

Ground plans of the dungeon and of the lower chamber. China ink drawing by Louzier, 1891 (Paris, Médiathèque du Patrimoine).

entation permits the surveillance of the main road leading into the city.

The quality of the architecture and decorative details of the **antechamber** that leads into the upper chamber are impressive: its entrance is a gothic arch flanked with colonnettes including two spans of pointed-barrel vaults and ribs with springs reposing upon four round colonnettes. The last span of the vestibule is brightened by a window. Secured access to the upper chamber was ensured by the panelled door and the murder-hole of the vestibule.

The layout of the **upper chamber** is identical to that of the lower, but with additional amenities. The annular keystone gives onto

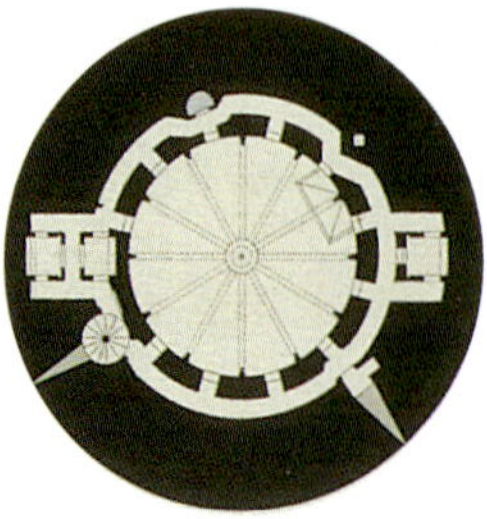

Ground plans of the annular passageway in the wall of the lower chamber. China ink drawing by Louzier, 1891 (Paris, Médiathèque du Patrimoine).

Vault and covered watchpath of the lower chamber and vault of the upper chamber.

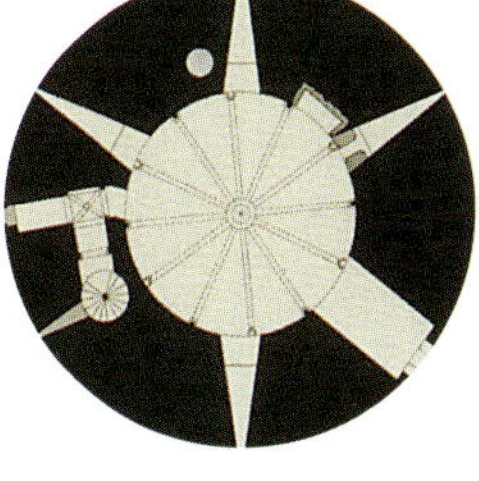

Ground plan of the lower chamber, by Louzier.

the terrace as on the other levels, where the open keystones give onto the level above. The upper chamber is equipped with a chimney and five arrow slits. The room once served as a prison, notably for Protestants in the 18th century; the embrasure of a loophole* was converted into a cell, another was enlarged into a rectangular chamber lit by a window. It is upon the ledge of the circular opening that one can find the famous inscription *Register* (Resist), attributed to the most renowned of the Protestant women prisoners, Marie Durand.

Graffiti, in the embrasure of a window in the vestibule, probably dating from the 13th century, featuring a boat with lateen sails.

Vault of the entrance-hall of the upper chamber.

There are other such inscriptions visible in the antechamber and in the embrasure of the window: the etched graffiti of five ships, two with lateen sails, probably dating to the 13th century.

The terrace has six loopholes*, currently walled-up but still visible from the exterior, the parapet having since been modified to support four embrasures for cannon. It is a natural strategic point for surveillance as the tower dominates the region.

Through a corkscrew staircase installed in the topmost turret, one reaches a circular passageway within the wall, where a metal lantern once held a fire which served as a beacon from medieval to modern times. It was from this tower that the town kept vigil for ships heading for the open sea.

Sources dating back to 1298-1299 yielded information about the diverse functions of the tower: "It was traditional, from the building of the tower up to the present day to have a keeper always present [...] and, whenever a ship passed within the vicinity of the town, he would sound a horn, or otherwise signal the warden of the port that a ship desired passage". Then it was a matter of collecting the levies and taxes due on the merchandise conveyed, notably the right claimed by the city to one denier per pound of merchandise transported, a tax originally created to finance the fortifications of the town. This tower is not open to the public.

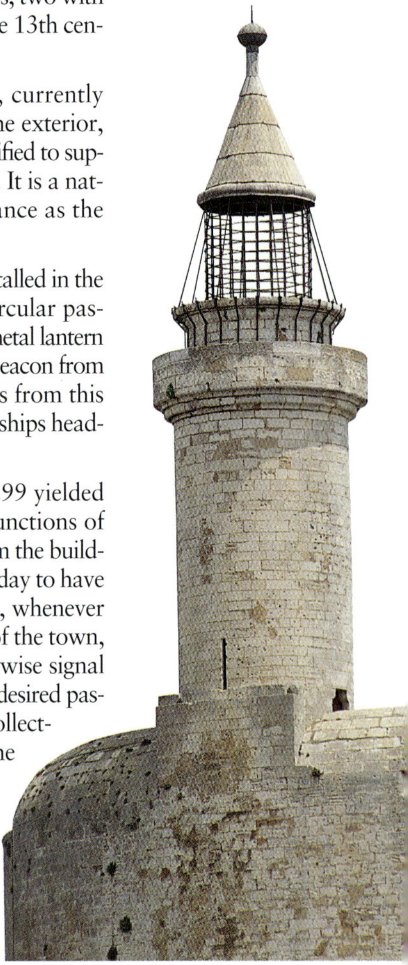

The Town Walls

Begun in 1272 and finished before the end of the 13th century, the town walls have had some minor reconstruction done and have been adapted for more modern weaponry over the years. The parapet of the Tour de Constance, the circumvallations surrounding the castle, the entrances to the castle and the tower were also modified. Today only the stone framework is visible; the wooden superstructure, specifically the hourdis (or wooden galleries) and the roofing, no longer exist.

Terrace of the Tour de Constance, with its parapet cleft by four embrasures for cannon and the turret with circular passageway and beacon.

The town wall is in the form of an irregular quadrilateral, with sides measuring 520, 325, 510 and 285 meters respectively. Fifteen outworks complete the fortifications: five large gates and five smaller ones, two flanking towers, and only three corner turrets since the northern defenses are assured by the imposing Tour de Constance.

The number, type and placing of the

outworks are not consistent from one side to another. Consequently, the southwest front has five points of entry, as opposed to only two on the northeast, which, being the side that faces inland and the sole road leading to the city, is more vulnerable. The defense of the north side is reinforced by two flanking towers, the Tour du Sel and the Tour de la Mèche and the lagoon which links the town with its port, as well as providing additional natural protection.

The northeast front of the Tour de la Mèche.

Linking the defensive outworks, the curtain-walls are eleven meters tall and two and a half meters thick. The exterior portion of the wall is shored up on a slant for better resistance and has two rows of arrow slits.

The covered watchpaths are placed in a chicane*, or baffle between the towers. Currently one is not obliged to cross them, except to gain access to the Tour de Sel and the smaller gateways.

One plan from the beginning of the 17th century shows the medieval fortifications doubled with a bastioned outer wall surrounding the Porte de la Gardette, the Porte de Saint-Antoine, the Porte de la Reine and the three corner towers. The two fortifications were surrounded by watered moats. Were these modifications completed? Nothing on 18th-century plans shows evidence of them; if they were indeed completed, they have since disappeared, as has the moat, except between the Tour des Bourguignons and the Porte des Moulins. In 1811, the fortifications were abandoned by the military authorities and the works were entered in the Register of Historical Monuments in 1903.

The southwest front of the Porte des Moulins and the Porte des Galions.

The bulk of the fortifications are constructed with filled bond with a facing done in hewn flagstones and bonding brick, alternating in height and width. The bricks are uniform in appearance, of average dimensions, square or rectangular, with more or less uniform bossage mingled with smooth mortared bond. The smaller mortar often gives way to a larger bond 0.35 meters thick, found more frequently in the upper layers of both the curtain-wall and the defensive outworks. This diversity of materials would perhaps indicate that construction occurred in several stages.

Many questions remain regarding the laying of the foundations, since there have been no

The Tour Carbonnière

Situated 3.5 kilometers from Aigues-Mortes, in what is today the commune of Saint-Laurent-d'Aigouze, the Tour Carbonnière rises up in the middle of the swampland, dominating the sole access to the city by land. The exact date of construction is unknown but it was undoubtedly finished at the beginning of the 14th century. It is a tower-gatehouse with a rectangular layout, comprising a barrel-vaulted passageway on the ground level with a double portcullis, a guard-room on the first floor, also barrel-vaulted, and an upper terrace which originally had turrets in each corner.

This tower was an integral part of the fortifications and defenses of Aigues-Mortes and is characteristic of such constructions.

The Tour Carbonnière, an independent edifice situated to the north of the city which formerly controlled access to the town by land.

archeological surveys. The existence of a foundation raft made of long paving stones 1.5 meters underground, upon which the footing* of the curtain-wall rests is known but the original foundations go even deeper.

The basic material utilized is a yellow ochre limestone. Its exact provenance is difficult to ascertain since similar characteristics are all to be found in the outcropping of the Burdigalien in the zone along the Languedoc plain between Beaucaire and Montpellier. Studies have nevertheless shown that the quarry of Aubais, located twenty-five kilometers from Aigues-Mortes, furnished much of the stone for the fortifications. But there is

Mason's Marks

We have yet to know the exact origin of these marks which occur frequently on the stones of fortifications and other constructions of the Middle Ages. There are over 600 to be found at Aigues-Mortes. Since masons were often paid by the amount of work they completed, the marks helped identify the author of the completed work. It is worth noting that the Tour de Constance is devoid of them; currently there is no satisfactory explanation for this.

Mason's marks visible in the limestone of the square and rectangular bricks, the smooth bond and on the bossage of the fortifications.

Alcove of a bi-level loophole, in curtain-wall VI.

a second stone used in the coping of the walls: a sandstone whose origins undoubtedly lie further to the northeast, in the Vaucluse or around Uzès.

The Fortifications

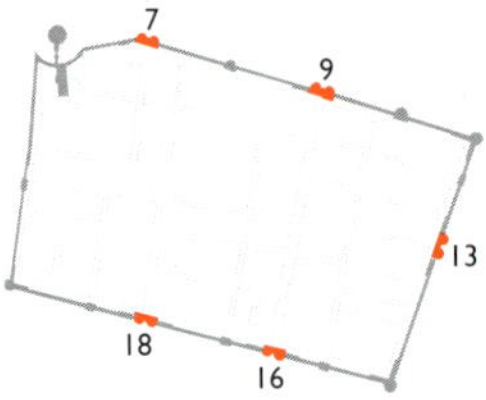

The defensive outworks, located astride the curtain-walls, consist of a covered terrace protected by machicolations* with one loophole* per merlon*. Three types of constructions are to be found.

The Greater Gatehouses, or "Portes"

The Porte de la Gardette[7], Porte de Saint-Antoine[9], Porte de la Reine[13], Porte de la Marine[16], Porte des Moulins[18]

The main body of the structure is rectangular, juxtaposed by two semi-circular watch turrets which extend town-side into rectangular massifs. The covered watchpath wends its way behind the turrets, connecting the curtain-walls on either side. The interior, or "military" stairways which lean upon the curtain-wall provide access from the town to the covered watchpath and issue from either extremity of the gatehouse.

The Porte de la Marine (southwest front on the town side), the Porte de la Gardette, Porte Saint Antoine (northeast front, both sides). Aquarelles by Louzier, 1889 (Paris, Médiathèque du Patrimoine).

The Fortifications

The names of the various structures all date from the modern period.

The Porte de la **Gardette** probably owes its name to the proximity of the guardhouse. Also referred to as the "Porte de Nimes" or simply the "Porte" (or Gate) as it quickly became the main means of entry into the city of Aigues-Mortes.

The Tour du **Sel** (or "Salt Tower"), also referred to as the "Military Prison Tower" is also thought to have served as a salt-house. The graffiti found in the lower chamber indicates that it was once used as a prison. The cemetery of **Saint-Antoine** is located just on the other side of the city limits. The former name of the Tour de **Villeneuve** was the "Tour des Masques," but the reason for the name is not known. The Porte des **Cordeliers** is named for the convent located close by and the Porte de la **Reine** to commemorate the visit of Anne of Austria, who visited Aigues-Mortes in 1622. The Tour de la **Poudrière** and the Porte de l'**Arsenal** are also thus dubbed because of the proximity of the stronghold's arsenal. The Porte de la **Marine** is the closest to the former port.

The Porte des **Moulins** was once possessed of two windmills. The Porte des **Galions** and the Porte de l'**Organeau**, were previously named the Porte du Portalet et de Thioule and Porte Tioulet et de Thieurre, respectively; these names are references to the proximity of the anchorage of the old port. The Tour des **Bourguignons** is so named for the traditional assertion that, in 1421, after the massacre of the Burgundian garrison, that the bodies of the soldiers were tossed into this tower…and salted in order to preserve them temporarily. The Porte des **Remblais** is the name given to the Porte de Montpellier after the filling-in (or remblaiment) of the moat.

On the ground level there is a sort of recess located between the two portcullises. Security is further assured by the presence of a murder-hole on the first level and from the lower chamber by two loopholes* installed in a recess of the wall. Three other arrow slits give off onto the surrounding countryside. The recess, entry hall and the spiral staircase are all located within the thickness of the surrounding wall. A double-panelled door secured these works, one panel shut off the city side and one the open countryside. The Porte de la Reine, the Porte de la Marine and the Porte des Moulins closely resemble each other in terms of interior amenities but the dimensions of the Porte de Saint-Antoine and the Porte de la Gardette are larger.

Sculpted keystone in the upper chamber, right tower of the Porte des Moulins.

Transverse cross-section of the Porte de la Marine. Aquarelle by Louzier, 1889 (Paris, Médiathèque du Patrimoine).

On the first level, the central chambers, square or rectangular in form, are covered by ribbed vaults with ornamental keystones. Access is gained through the covered watchpath on the posterior façade — the lateral façade in the case of the Porte de la Reine and the Porte des Moulins. A ribbed vault with six spandrels covers the upper chambers.

The terraces are similar, with three or four arrow slits on the city side and six or seven facing outward. The stairwell opens onto the access corridor leading to the lower chamber — in the case of the Porte de la Reine, the Porte des Moulins and the Porte de la Marine; or it is recessed into the lateral massif at the juncture with the curtain-wall — as in the case of the Porte de Saint-Antoine and the Porte de la Gardette.

Upstairs chimney in the Porte Saint Antoine. Aquarelle by Louzier, 1889 (Paris, Médiathèque du Patrimoine).

The latrines of the lower chambers are accessible by covered watchpaths. Some — notably

The ribbed vaulting in one of the rooms in the Porte de la Marine.

Double page, overleaf:

The Porte des Cordeliers (Southeast front, both sides), the Tour de Villeneuve (corner of the northeast and southeast fronts, city side). Aquarelles by Louzier, 1889 and 1891 (Paris, Médiathèque du Patrimoine).

the Porte de la Marine — open onto the stairwells, others are laid out within the massif of the towers on the outer side.

The spaces are lit by several rectangular windows facing out onto the countryside and, at the Porte de la Reine, additionally complemented by an arrow slit in each turret. Chimneys are present at every level.

A floor covered the lower chambers of the Porte des Moulins and the Porte de la Marine; the presence of several wooden devices are also indicated by marks on the wall but their nature and function remains a mystery.

The layout of the Porte de la Reine stands out amongst the uniformity of the whole. At the extremities of the terrace, two square watch turrets are accessed by the corkscrew staircase that unites the whole. They contain two superimposed chambers covered by a ribbed vault under the terrace. These were probably additional reinforcements, designed to afford greater protection to the curtain-wall.

The first level and the terraces of the Porte de la Marine and the Porte des Moulins are accessible and one can also view the ground level of the Porte de la Gardette (which houses the Office of Tourism).

Decoration of the Structures

Gargoyle with lion's head.

The keystones, the bottoms of the springers of the vaulted arches, and some gargoyles form the totality of a decorative scheme which lacks any specific coherence. Still, a satirical quality can be discerned in the whole: many figures are possessed of common attributes, such as cowls and various types of headgear which are much in evidence and are symbolic of a crude definition of social stratification and the grotesque caricatures evident in the postures and the exaggeration of various physical traits are further examples of this tendency. The themes are varied: beasts, fighting monsters or androphagi dominate the lower part of the city walls, which have few floral details—in contrast to the keystones, which are sometimes historiated. The gargoyles are mostly straight out of the bestiary, with a scattering of human figures.

The Smaller Gatehouses

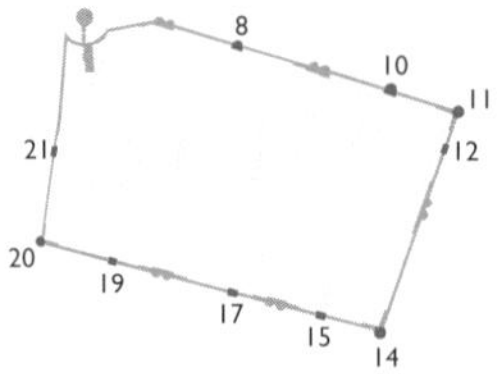

The Porte des Cordeliers[12], Porte de l'Arsenal[15], Porte des Galions[17], Porte de l'Organeau[19], and Porte des Remblais[21]

Rectangular in shape, they intersect the fortifications and are composed of a ground level, a chamber on the first floor with a ribbed vault, covered with a terrace defined by four turrets, one of which holds the stairwell. A portcullis and murder-hole complete the whole. In the upper chamber, the vault is pierced by a trap door which leads to the balcony, which was either used as a supply pulley or to control the portcullis.

The turrets are decorative. There are two variations distinguishable in the work as a whole. All of the smaller gatehouses are accessible, with the exception of the Porte de l'Organeau and the Porte des Remblais.

Vault of the upstairs chamber of the Porte des Cordeliers.

The Flanking Towers

The Tour du Sel[8] and the Tour de la Mèche[10]

As seen from outside the city walls, they offer a semi-circular aspect, with two chambers, one above the other, with ribbed vaulting and a terrace. Communication between the gangways is accomplished by an exterior covered watchpath which passes behind the upper chamber, or through the upper chamber itself.

The stairs are located in the exterior wall. A window which gives onto the city lights the lower chamber. Each chamber is fitted with a fireplace. The chambers and terraces of the gatehouses are accessible.

Upper part of the Porte des Cordeliers, on the southeast front, facing out of the city.

The Corner Towers

The Tour de Villeneuve[11], the Tour de la Poudrière[14], and the Tour des Bourguignons[20]

These structures juxtapose a semi-circular plan with a polygonal space. The lower chamber, circular in form, is accessible through a door from the *rue militaire* and the upper chamber, also in a circular layout, is entered through the covered watchpath, the posterior façade, or by the right flank, as in the Tour des Bourguignons. The stairwell is carved out of the fortress wall. The chambers have ribbed vaults and walls pierced with arrow slits, some of which have been converted into gun-sites.

Keystone of the upstairs chamber of the Tour du Sel, on the northeast front.

Only the Tour des Bourguignons has a window and a fireplace on the ground level (visible throughout the level). Defense is handled through loopholes*: five in the lower chamber (only three in the Tour des Bourguignons), five to seven on the terrace. The numbers in the upper chamber are more irregular, in particular in the Tour de Villeneuve, which only

Upstairs chamber of the Tour du Sel.

has one of the six originally intended. Access to the upper chamber was monitored through a murder-hole accessed through the terrace. Only the Tour de Villeneuve is accessible on the first level and the terrace.

The Town

Double page, overleaf: Panoramic view featuring the bells of Notre-Dame-des-Sablons and the Place Saint-Louis along with the southwest front of the ramparts, the Étang de Psalmodi and the salt marshes.

After having entered through the Porte de la Gardette, one comes upon the Place d'Armes and the Governor's Residence through which one enters the Tour de Constance and the ramparts. Upon leaving the Residence, take a right on the principal street, Rue Jean-Jaurès, or Grande-Rue; then, after pausing at the Church of Notre-Dame-des-Sablons, make your way to the Place Saint-Louis where you can observe the statue of Louis IX, the town

hall, and the chapel of the Capuchin convent. In the eastern part of the city, you can catch sight of the Chapelle des Pénitents Blancs, the Chapelle des Pénitents Gris and a few other older dwellings.

The 13th-century fortifications enclose the city within an irregular quadrilateral of sixteen hectares with streets cut at right angles. The fortifications are made up of ten gatehouses, five of which are equipped with two watch turrets, as well as six independent towers, interspersed with sixteen curtain-walls along a perimeter of 1.62 kilometers. An esplanade five to ten meters in width, initially designed to ease movement for the garrison, runs along the interior; it facilitates a tour of the walls, except between the Porte de la Gardette and the Tour du Sel, where, for many years, a private encroachment has impeded access.

1
2 | 3
4

There are roughly three areas discernible: the first, to the north, bordered by the Rue Jean-Jaurès and the Boulevard Gambetta; the second, at the end of the Rue Jean-Jaurès, comprising the Place Saint-Louis — the veritable heart of the city — located between the northeast and southwest walls of the city; the third is in the south, formed by the Rue Émile-Jamais and the Rue Sadi-Carnot, with a east-west axis located between the Porte de la Reine and the Porte des Remblais.

At n° 2 **Rue Jean-Jaurès,** is a large residence, now in a rather dilapidated state, with large windows topped with curved frontons; a set of nine corbels* of limestone decorated with male and female heads embellish the façade. Nos 7 and 19 on the same street are early 17th-century houses which were extensively renovated in the 19th century and have façades ornamented with corbels* and grooved pilasters with sculpted capitals.

The church of **Notre-Dame-des-Sablons**[23], mentioned in sources as early as 1260, is a structure comprising three naves with five bays and a flat end apse. It was constructed before the fortifications, during the lifetime of Louis IX and completed in the 15th century when lateral chapels were placed between the buttresses. It suffered the vicissitudes of various religious conflicts throughout history: it was vandalized in 1575, then its bell tower was reconstructed during the 17th and 18th

centuries. Converted into a grain shop, then a salt-house, it was finally reconsecrated at the beginning of the last century and underwent restoration thirty years ago. The stained glass windows in the interior are the work of Claude Viallat, a contemporary artist from Nimes.

The **Place Saint-Louis**[22] has always been at the center of city life, if not at the actual center of town. It is actually centered on the western half of the city. This curious disposition is explained by the stages of the construction of Aigues-Mortes: the city was founded in 1240, but the surrounding fortifications were not begun until 1272. If there are some disparities between the regular disposition of the streets and the less regular layout of the surrounding walls, it might be imputed more to the respecting of former constructions and public streets, as well as to geographical obstructions, such as the presence of a lagoon and a *roubine*. The question remains to be answered.

A first town hall is mentioned in sources dating back to the creation of the town in the 13th century; it was reconstructed in the 16th century. The current edifice dates back to the 17th century; its façade was totally redone in the 19th century, as well as its interior, with the exception of the stairwell.

Along the south side of the square sits the former **convent of the Capuchin monastery**[24], founded in 1622 in order to facilitate the conversion of Protestants. Today, it is a gallery. Pierced by a large arcade topped by a roundel*, its façade gives off onto a sole rectangular vessel.

Commissioned by the city of Aigues-Mortes to commemorate the Seventh and Eighth Crusades, **the statue of Louis IX** which occupies the centre of the square was completed in 1849 by the sculptor James Pradier.

One comes upon several objects of architectural interest along the various streets — notably at n°s 19-25 of the Rue de la République, n°s 16, 26 and 28 Rue Émile-Jamais as well as at n°s 23 and 35 of Boulevard Gambetta. But the oldest residence is probably that at n° 6 of the Rue Paul-Bert, a small rectangular 16th-century building of one storey with a timbered roof. It has the added attraction of a gable wall which was formerly a façade giving onto

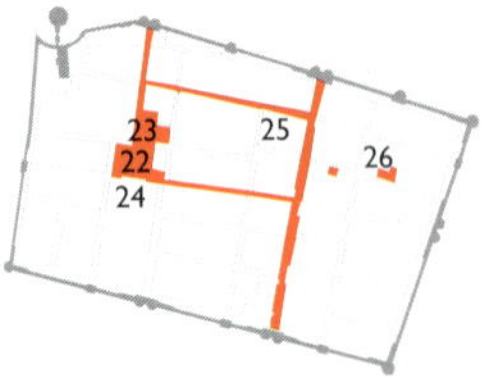

The Chapelle de la Confrérie des Pénitents Gris on the Rue Rouget-de-l'Isle.

the street and, on the first floor, you can perceive the remains of a window with a dripstone* over it.

The Chapelle des **Pénitents Gris**[26] is located on Rue Rouget-de-l'Isle. It was a lay confraternity whose presence here seems to date back to the 15th century. In 1575, during the Wars of Religion, the original chapel was destroyed and a new one was consecrated in 1611. It is a church with a single nave and a flat end apse, with a neighbouring dwelling built along the lines of the Chapelle des Pénitents Blancs.

The Chapelle des **Pénitents Blancs**[25], on the Rue de la République, is a fairly simple building, also built around a single nave with a semi-circular apse. Created by a schism amongst the Grey Penitents, this lay confraternity was founded in the 17th century, the probable date of construction of the chapel. It was the seat of the Revolutionary Committee of Aigues-Mortes, when its archives were destroyed. In the 19th century, the confraternity, which has survived to this day, has begun to restore the chapel and its furnishings.

These two buildings can be visited by formally requesting permission from the Aigues-Mortes Tourist Office at the Porte de la Gardette.

1
Place Saint-Louis, with the statue of Louis IX and the façade of the church of the former Capuchin convent.

2
Sixteenth-century house, located at n° 6 of the Rue Paul-Bert.

3-4
Houses with ornamental façades, n°s 19 and 2, of the Rue Jean-Jaurès.

Fronton over the portal of the Chapelle de la Confrérie des Pénitents Blancs, on the Rue de la République.

Glossary

Barbican, or outwork: an outer defense to a city or castle, specifically a double tower erected over a gate or bridge.

Barrel vault: a vault with a roof of uniform concave structure.

Bartizan: a battlemented parapet at the top of a fortification or castle.

Bastide: a fortified village or town.

Bond: the jointing or fastening of masonry; any of various methods of holding a wall together by making bricks overlap.

Bossage: projecting stonework as ornamentation on a wall or to affix sculptures, or bosses.

Chicane: or baffle, a zigzag passage that one is obliged to take to access a secured area in a fortification.

Corbel: also console or bracket; a projecting moulding serving as a support.

Corkscrew staircase: a spiral staircase constructed upon a single axis.

Curtain-wall: portion of a fortress wall which connects two bastions, towers, gates, or similar structures.

Dripstone: a weather moulding designed to keep rain off the wall.

Dungeon, or oubliette: a strong subterranean cell for prisoners, a deep, dark vault.

Gothic arch: a pointed arch, characteristic of the Gothic architectural style of the Middle Ages.

Governor: in the Middle Ages, a town, or municipal magistrate, the official in charge of town administration.

Hourdis: a wooden gallery constructed on top of a fortress wall, with openings in the floor for launching projectiles.

Keep: also donjon, the principal tower of a castle.

Lateen sail: a triangular sail.

Lido: offshore bar enclosing a lagoon.

Loophole, or arrow slit: a narrow, vertical slit in a wall, for shooting or looking through.

Machicolation: the opening in a projecting wall or parapet through which pitch or molten lead might be cast upon the enemy beneath.

Merlon: the solid part of an embattled parapet between two embrasures.

Murder-hole: an opening in the keystone or ceiling which enables the beseiged to cast projectiles upon the enemy.

Parapet: a low wall or barrier at the edge of a balcony or roof or along a rampart.

Pilaster: a rectangular column, especially one projecting from the wall, also, formerly the square pier of an arch.

Portcullis: a barrier in the form of a grating of wooden or iron bars, usually suspended by chains over the gateway of a fortress, able to be quickly released to slide down and secure the entrance.

Raft: a facing or casing serving as a foundation.

Roundel: or oculus, a round window.

Sloped footing: a curved, thickened base (of a tower or fortification) designed to improve stability.

Sorbel: base jutting forth from a wall; generally sculpted.

Watchpath: passageway constructed within the thickness of a wall.

A short bibliography

Aigues-Mortes

Pagézy (Jules), *Mémoires sur le port d'Aigues-Mortes,* Paris, 1879-1886, 2 vol.

Sablou (Jean), "Saint Louis et le problème de la fondation d'Aigues-Mortes", in *Hommage à André Dupont. Études médiévales languedociennes,* Montpellier, 1974, p. 255-265.

Saint Louis

Le Goff (Jacques), *Saint Louis,* Paris, Gallimard, "Bibliothèque des histoires" series, 1996.

Richard (Jean), *Saint Louis, roi d'une France féodale, soutien de la Terre sainte,* Paris, 1983 (reprint, 1986).

The Crusades

Delor (Robert), ed., *Les Croisades,* Paris, Seuil, "Points-Histoire" series, n° 100, 1988.

Grousset (René), *Histoire des croisades et du royaume franc de Jérusalem,* Paris, 1934-1936, 3 vol. (reprint, Paris, 1992).

Tate (Georges), *L'Orient des croisades,* Paris, Gallimard, coll. "Découvertes-Histoire" series, n° 129, 1991.

Architecture

Canton d'Aigues-Mortes (Gard), Ministère des Affaires culturelles, Inventaire général des monuments et des richesses artistiques de la France, commission du Languedoc-Roussillon, Paris, Imprimerie nationale, 1973, 2 vol.

Fino (Jean-François), *Forteresses de la France médiévale, construction, attaque, défense,* Paris, 1970 (3e ed., 1977).

Sournia (Bernard), "Les fortifications d'Aigues-Mortes", *Congrès archéologique,* CXXXIV, 1976, p. 9-26.

Id., *Aigues-Mortes,* Paris, Caisse nationale des monuments historiques et des sites, "Petites notes sur les grands édifices" series, 1981.

Id., *Aigues-Mortes,* Rennes, Ouest-France/Caisse nationale des monuments historiques et des sites, 1994.